The Wit and Wisdom of West Highland Terriers

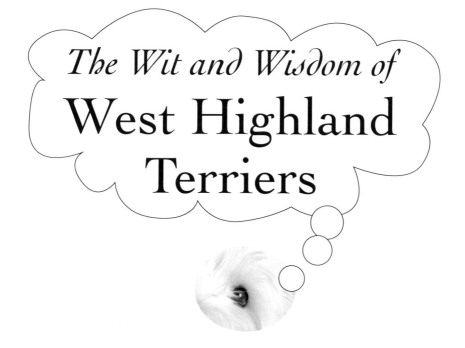

This is a STAR FIRE book

STAR FIRE BOOKS
Crabtree Hall, Crabtree Lane
Fulham, London SW6 6TY
United Kingdom

www.star-fire.co.uk

First published 2007

07 09 11 10 08

1 3 5 7 9 10 8 6 4 2

Star Fire is part of The Foundry Creative Media Company Limited

© The Foundry 2007

The CIP record for this book is available from the British Library.

ISBN: 978 1 84451 806 7

Printed in China

Thanks to: Cat Emslie, Andy Frostick, Sara Robson,
Gemma Walters and Nick Wells

The Wit and Wisdom of West Highland Terriers

Ulysses Brave

STAR FIRE

Foreword

For years I studied Zen and the Art of
Animal Self-consciousness. Subsequently I
have written a large number of management,
self-help and philosophical texts over the
years, which have provided helpful advice
to those less fortunate than myself.
Here then, is my latest offering.

Ulysses Brave

Try to keep your head up if you're feeling low. Apart from keeping the hair from your eyes, it will instill confidence.

Confidence is the key to success. When hunting for friends or jobs, always walk with a ready smile and a straight back.

*Try to avoid situations
which you find depressing.*

Make some time every
day to celebrate.

Fear is your greatest enemy. You can defeat it by remembering those who love you.

If you have trouble concentrating, just take five deep breaths and remain still for two minutes.

Be ready for action at all times, especially in the defence of your places of rest.

Sometimes the perfect colour
is simply not available.
Try not to put yourself
under too much pressure.

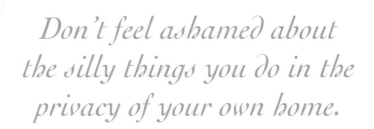

Don't feel ashamed about the silly things you do in the privacy of your own home.

Twins can be fun.

Curiosity can be a good thing.
Judgement is always better.

If life seems to become entangled, try to do something completely different.

*There are times when we
all want to sink into the
background. Camouflage,
correctly administered,
can be useful.*

Here we go again...

Opening your lungs first thing in the morning will fill your body with life-enhancing energy.

The ancient art of moon-staring
can bring significant benefits
to the inner soul.

*Luxuries and privileges
can sometimes hold you back.
It is often better to fight for
what you want.*

Just focus on your goals...

...dont wait for events, leap towards them and wrestle them to the ground.

Going to a party can relieve the tension, even if it's the last thing you want to do.

Some people like parties!

*Try to maintain
a healthy diet.*

If you bring a friend to an important event, make sure they don't cramp your style.

Watch and compose yourself before you leap in. Success lies in planning and poise.

Dreaming of a better place can help you through the day.

Sometimes it's a great relief
to get to the end of the day.

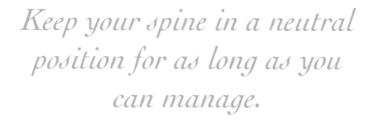

Keep your spine in a neutral position for as long as you can manage.

*Try to leave the city
behind for a few hours
a week.*

Some people will be wary if you show too much enthusiasm.

Try to find a new challenge in your life.

If you find yourself in a tight corner, genuine curiosity can be the most disarming weapon.

All forms of Martial Arts provide great discipline.

You know a true friend
by their attitude to
your appearance.

See you soon...